First-time Home Buying

In a Nutshell

by Greg Urata

Information in this document is subject to change without notice. Rules and regulations within and for the industry change on a regular basis. This information is general and not specific as different localities may have regulations and laws distinct to their location. It may not, however, be appropriate for analysis of your particular transaction due to differences in accounting principles, tax laws and other regulations and standards applicable in your area. No part of this document may be reproduced or transmitted in any form or by any means, electronic or mechanical, for any purpose, without the express permission of Greg Urata.

DEDICATION

To my entire family and friends whose love and support makes my life fulfilled.

CONTENTS

Introduction

(Important to read before continuing)

This book is intended to offer the reader a primer and quick reference guide to the home buying and loan process, not to make you a real estate expert or take the place of using a professional agent. Generally, you don't have to pay a buyer's agent from your own pocket. The seller usually pays the listing agent and the listing agent splits the commission with the buyer's agent.

Having been in the real estate business since 1988 and lending since 1991 I've learned that most first-time home buyers have no idea how the whole process works. I have finally decided to write this so that the home buyer will be armed with the basic aspects of buying a home and not feel like they are flailing around in the dark during the entire process.

Due to the culture we are living in, most information is doled out in short phrases or "sound bites". Therefore, I wrote this in "sound bites" by giving just enough information on any given subject for you to have a basic understanding. If you want to pursue it further you have that option. Go to www.thenutshellbook.com for links to additional information.

Ultimately, you should rely on your real estate agent and loan officer for guidance because all the nuances and eccentricities of each transaction require someone who is experienced and thoroughly knowledgeable. Each state has its own rules and regulations as well as smaller municipalities such as counties and cities. This book is meant to give a general view and vocabulary regarding these processes and not necessarily applicable in all areas of the country. Again, this is why it is important to have a professional assist you through the home buying process.

Contained in this book is a section on down payment assistance programs. If you feel that you might meet the low to moderate income threshold and you would be interested in down payment assistance it is critical that you find a loan officer who has experience in these types of loans as they can be far more difficult to analyze and process than a normal type of loan. Most down payment assistance programs require that the loan officer and lender go through a certification process.

There are also loans that allow funds to rehabilitate a property. An FHA 203K loan is one of these types of loans. At the time of writing this book there is also a loan called the Neighborhood Stabilization Program (NSP). Some municipalities allow rehab with the NSP loan.

In addition I placed into the appendix some items that you might need to know such as a list of the different types of housing and different types of loans you may run into. There is also a typical list of documents that you will need to supply your loan officer with to do the loan.

Finally, there is a section on definitions designed <u>not</u> to go into too much detail but to give you only what you need to know and rely on your agent and loan officer for the nuances. In some instances I will use the acronym followed by the actual phrase. It depends on which is used more so it will be easier to find such as "FHA". Very few people say "The Federal Housing Administration".

You can go to <u>www.thenutshellbook.com</u> for links to additional information and sites with down payment assistance and first-time home buyer programs from cities, counties, states, and Federal government.

(If you have additional questions that are not covered by this book, feel free to email the author at <u>gurata@cox.net</u>.)

CHAPTER 1

Beginning the Home Buying Process

1) Getting Loan Approval

Find a good loan officer, preferably someone who is recommended to you. You will need a pre-qualification or a pre-approval before you start looking for a property so you know what you can afford. (See section on loans)

2) Finding a Buyer's Agent

An experienced buyer's agent is worth his/her weight in gold in this market. It's best to get someone who has been recommended to you by a friend or relative and is knowledgeable about the areas in which you are looking. The author's recommendation is to find someone who has been working in real estate for at least one year and has sold, on their own, at least three or four properties. As was stated in the introduction, generally, you don't have to pay a buyer's agent from your own pocket. The seller usually pays the listing agent and the listing agent splits the commission with the buyer's agent.

Because most of the homes for sale these days are either foreclosures or short sales, an agent must know how to navigate all the pitfalls in dealing with bank owned properties. Banks do not negotiate as though this is a buyer's market. They have been known to demand more than normal conditions before accepting an offer. Your agent will explain these to you as they differ with individual banks and locales.

3) Finding a Home

A good agent will be knowledgeable about the areas in which you are looking. They will search through the MLS (Multiple Listing Service) for homes that match your criteria.

Your agent can also place you on what is called "Gateway®". This is a service of the MLS (Multiple Listing Service) which will automatically email you a list of properties that meet your criteria in the area in which you are looking. It will also send you the new listings that meet your criteria as soon as they come on the market. You will be able to see pictures and descriptions and important details of the properties.

Trying to get a list of foreclosures (often called REOs [real estate owned]) directly from a bank or make an offer on a foreclosure to the bank is generally futile. (This does not necessarily apply to smaller, locally-owned banks and credit unions) The majority of large banks use independent/autonomous law firms to handle the complex matters that are involved in foreclosures and then the law firms distribute the properties to various real estate brokers with whom they have an established relationship. You will generally see the foreclosures on the MLS once they have been distributed to the listing brokers.

Be wary of auctions because their rules can be very complex. If you do not know or understand the rules you could lose thousands of dollars, through penalties and commissions, even if you do not actually complete the buying process.

4)   Writing a Purchase Offer

Once you find a property that fits your criteria your agent will write up a purchase offer. You will need to provide a good faith deposit. The amount of the good faith deposit depends upon the norm for your area. There could also be a counteroffer phase if the seller does not like certain aspects of your offer.

Your agent will do a comparable market analysis to make sure that what you are offering is not above the actual market value of the property.

You will need to have a fully executed purchase contract (agreed to and signed by all parties including the bank on a short sale) before you can lock the interest rate and open escrow.

Your agent will explain the disposition and the risk potential of your good faith deposit. States have different rules regarding the return of the deposit if the sale does not go through to closing.

5) Opening Escrow

Escrow is a service that collects all of the documentation, invoices, contracts, agreements, funds, etc. It acts as a clearing house and central coordinating entity to make sure all paperwork and funds are dispersed properly.

While in escrow you will have a certain length of time (contingency period), depending on what you have agreed to in the purchase offer, in which to do your due diligence and release contingencies. Some of these items include termite/pest inspection, property inspection, pool inspection, appraisal, loan approval, research of the area's schools and crime statistics, etc.

Chapter 2 will list and briefly explain the highlights in the escrow process.

CHAPTER 2

The Escrow Process

1) Getting the Purchase Agreement

After all parties to the contract have signed, the agent will open escrow and submit the contract to escrow. Some states use lawyers in lieu of escrow to process the transaction. This author is not familiar with how the transaction is handled in those states.

2) Escrow Instructions

Escrow will create escrow instructions outlining the specifics of the transaction.

3) Preliminary Title

Escrow will order a preliminary title report. A preliminary title report is a document that outlines information that is pertinent to the property such as easements, liens, encumbrances, etc that might compromise free and clear title to the property. It is important for buyers to review this document to make sure they are not going to unknowingly encumber themselves through buying the property.

4) Estimated HUD 1

This is a document that lists the preliminary financial accounting of the costs and financing amounts of the transaction. There is a final HUD 1/Settlement Statement issued at the end of the escrow process to show the final costs and financing amounts of the transaction.

5) Payoff Demand

This is a request made by escrow to the current mortgage holder of the existing loan(s) on the property for the total amount due to pay off the loan.

6) Drawing Docs

The process in which the buyer's lender prepares the documents (loan contract) to be sent to escrow to be signed by the buyer. Escrow usually reviews the documents to ensure they are accurate.

7) Signing Docs

When the loan documents are signed by the buyer in escrow (or by the lender) witnessed by a notary.

8) Funding

The signed documents are returned to the lender and the lender then funds the loan by sending funds to the title company which, in turn, sends the proceeds to escrow for disbursement.

9) Record and Close

After funding, the title company records the title at the
County Recorder's Office.

CHAPTER 3
The Loan Process

1) Submitting the Loan Application

When applying for a loan a form is filled out called the Uniform Residential Loan Application or 1003 form. The information on this form will be used to qualify the borrower for the loan.

2) Pre-qualification vs. Pre-approval

A pre-qualification (pre-qual) is a loan qualification which uses financial information about the borrower obtained verbally from the borrower and which has not been substantiated by documentation. This is usually used to preliminarily determine if the borrower should be taken to the next step of pre-approval and to approximate how much the borrower can afford in order to buy a house.

A pre-approval is when a credit report has been pulled and supporting documents have been used to qualify the borrower for a loan.

Qualifying is primarily based on, but not limited to:

- A ratio between your gross income per month and the amount of monthly debt/housing payment service (DTI).
- Credit Score (FICO®)
- Loan to Value (LTV) (What portion of the value of the home is financed)

3) Submitting the Supporting Documents

In order for the lender to determine if the borrower is in fact qualified for the loan the borrower must supply the lender with appropriate documents such as tax returns, W2s, paystubs, bank statements, etc. that will substantiate his/her financial condition. (See list of supporting documents in appendix)

4) Underwriting

An underwriter is someone who knows and understands all of the rules and regulations required by the government and lender to allow the loan to go through to funding. The underwriter goes through all the aspects of the loan and documents and verifies that the borrower does in fact meet all of the requirements.

5) Processing

Processing is when a processor gathers all the proper information, appraisal, and documentation in order to submit them to the underwriter for final approval. The processor interacts with the borrower, vendors, loan officer, real estate agents, escrow officer, property management company/HOA, and title officer in order to obtain all the information needed to complete the transaction.

6) Locking the Rate

This enables you to lock the interest rate for a specific period of time allowing you to be sure that you are getting the rate you are comfortable with. Rates can change several times a day so it is wise to ask the loan officer about trends and advice on when you should lock. No one can accurately predict what the lowest rate will be within a certain time period so don't expect it from your loan officer. It's always just an educated guess. Always ask the loan officer how long the rate is locked for. Extensions to the lock are usually possible for an additional fee.

7) Draw Docs

The process of creating the loan contract/documents for signature after the underwriter determines that all loan guidelines have been met.

8) Closing Costs

Escrow will provide a HUD 1 statement or closing statement to the borrower and seller to list the costs and indicate the closing costs the borrower/seller must pay at close escrow.

9) Sign Docs

The loan documents are usually signed in escrow by a notary public and then sent back to the lender for funding. Under certain conditions and circumstances the loan documents may be signed at the lender's office or at home by a notary.

10) Funding

This is when the lender sends the funds to the title company which in turn sends the funds to escrow for distribution to the appropriate entities.

11) Recording

After funding the title company records the sale at the County Recorder's Office, the transaction is complete and the buyer gets the keys.

CHAPTER 4
Down Payment Assistance

Most of the down payment assistance programs (DAP), also called first-time home buyer programs, are offered by local governments such as cities, counties, and states. However, some states with smaller populations offer DAPs rather than the local municipalities. Most DAPs are for first-time homebuyers (defined by not having owned a property within the last 3 years) that have household incomes below the area medium income (AMI) amounts. Most are limited to incomes at 80% of the AMI. AMI varies by geographic locations and can be found on the HUD website at: http://www.huduser.org/DATASETS/il/il09/index.html

When interested in a DAP it is best to have a loan officer who specializes in these types of loans. Most jurisdictions require that the loan officer and lender be certified by that jurisdiction to submit those loans. Not all loan officers will do DAPs because the total loan amounts are usually smaller and they require a lot more time and paperwork.

You can find out about DAPs in your area by going to your city, county, or state website. If you find it difficult to locate it on the website you can do a search within that website or look in the "sitemap" of that website and it will usually give you the link. Most DAPs require that you take a first-time homebuyer's seminar. A majority of the websites will have a list of approved lenders and loan officers.

Many of the DAPs will allow some of the funds to be used for closing costs (see definition). They often require a minimum amount of the down payment to be paid by the borrower such as 1% or 3% of the purchase price.

These DAPs are usually in the form of a second loan which is subordinate to the first loan. These are generally "silent seconds" which means that they do not require a monthly payment for the life of the loan (usually 30yrs) but either accrue simple interest and is payable at the end of the loan period or there is a participation in the equity increase of the house. Another way can be in the form of a grant which is forgiven if the borrower lives in the home for a specified length of time.

DAPs can often be more than just a down payment. They can be of substantial amounts to allow the buyer to qualify to purchase a home of higher value without increasing their monthly payments. For example, let's say that you qualify for a purchase of $100,000 without a DAP. The DAP offers up to $35,000 as a "silent second". You could feasibly buy a home for up to $135,000 at the same monthly payment as a $100,000 home.

There is another form of assistance that is called the

"Mortgage Credit Certificate" (MCC). This is a local program which is subsidized by the Federal Government. The terms vary by city or state but it is a Federal tax credit and reduces your withholding by a certain percentage of the monthly interest charge on the loan. Most local municipalities offer a 15% to 20% credit of the monthly interest charged on the loan. (At a 20% credit on a $1,000 monthly interest charge it would equal a $200 reduction in borrower's monthly withholding)

A website you can go to for a more in-depth explanation is www.ahahousing.com. This is a site for San Diego County but will give an explanation of the program.

(All of this information must be verified by the individual borrower's CPA or tax accountant. This author is not a tax expert and does not guarantee any of the above information and it is not intended as offering tax advice.)

Definitions of Terms Used in Real Estate and Lending

The definitions listed below are by no means complete or in-depth. These definitions are designed to make it easier to understand the basics of these terms thereby making it as simple as possible to understand those things a buyer/ borrower needs to know to make responsible decisions. We encourage the buyer/ borrower to research and learn as much as possible by reading more comprehensive and in-depth books or on the web on the subjects of loans and of buying real estate.

Accelerated Payment: These are types of programs offered by the lender to pay off the loan sooner than the maturity date.

Alienation Clause: A clause in the loan that states that if the owner sells or transfers title to the property the lender can call the loan as immediately due and payable. Almost all loans have this clause.

Amortize: (See Fully Amortized)

Appraisal: An opinion of the value of a property stated by a professional appraiser. There are three basic types:

1) Walk-in/Full: Actually entering the property and inspecting, viewing, measuring, and using comparable sales and/or construction costs to determine market value.

2) Drive-by: Driving by property to make sure that it exists and using comparable properties to determine value.

3) Desktop/Automated (AVM): Analyzed solely by using comparable sales of properties to determine value.

APR (Annual Percentage Rate): This is a combination of the actual note rate plus the costs of doing the loan expressed as an annual percentage rate. Even at the same note rate the APR might be different from lender to lender due to differences in costs such as broker fees and other lender fees.

Assumability: The ability of a loan to allow a person(s) other than those on the existing loan to "take over" the loan and "assume" the responsibility for repaying the loan and replace the current borrowers on the loan.

Balloon Payment: This is when the entire balance on a loan is due in one lump sum before the fully amortized loan date (maturity). These are generally agreed upon at the origination of the loan but can be called for by a lender if the borrower does not live up to the loan agreement.

Binder: A document from an insurer providing temporary insurance that states that, pending further investigation, they intend to issue a full insurance policy on a particular property.

Broker: A person who is authorized to act as an intermediary between two or more parties. There are usually rules and regulations regarding the acts and fiduciary (see definition below) responsibilities to those parties. In a real estate transaction the types of brokers that may be involved are the real estate broker, loan broker, and insurance broker. Real estate brokers may have agents working under their broker's license. Loan brokers may have loan officers working under their license.

Buy Down: The ability to pay an additional sum of money (points) to lower the interest rate.

Buyer's Agent: A real estate agent (Realtor®) that represents the buyer's interest in a transaction.

Buyer's Market: A market where there are more sellers than buyers usually resulting in prices going down.

Cash-out: When a borrower refinances his/her current mortgage for more than the actual loan amount to be paid off and uses the remainder for some other use such as repairs, renovations, or other loan payoffs.

Census Tracts: Demographic areas that have similar economic characteristics as determined by the Bureau of the Census.

Certificate of Eligibility: A Veteran's Administration document that is required in order for a veteran to be able to get a loan through the VA.

Closing Costs: These are the total fees from the lender, and other third parties such as escrow, title, appraisal, inspectors, termite, hazard insurance, home warranty insurance, property taxes, pre-paid interest, etc. that the buyer/seller must pay at close of escrow.

Co-borrower (co-signer): Someone who is an additional signer to the loan such as a spouse or someone added to the loan when the borrower's income or credit score is too low to qualify for a loan. The person added to the loan must be able to qualify in all aspects which an original borrower must qualify. The co-borrower must show that they can qualify for their current rent or mortgage payment as well as their portion of the new mortgage.

Compound Interest: Interest calculated as a percentage of both principal and accumulated unpaid interest.

Conditions: Issues such as documentation and finance that need to be met before a loan can be funded.

Condo Cert: It is necessary for a lender to approve a condo complex. There are many factors which could affect the eligibility of a condo to be lent upon. (e.g.: how many owners vs. how many investors own condos in the complex, if there is any pending litigation against the complex, if there are too many HOA dues in delinquency, etc.) The condo cert is a questionnaire required by the lender to be filled out by the property management company or the home owner's association concerning specific facts about the condo complex necessary for lender approval of the complex.

Construction Loan: A loan which is used just for the construction phase of a property which may include the purchase of the land depending on the guidelines of the lender.

Contingencies: Issues outlined in a purchase contract that need to be released by a given date in order for the purchase to move forward to closing. (e.g.: appraisal, loan approval, inspections, etc.)

Conversion Option: The option to convert the loan from an adjustable rate mortgage to a fixed rate mortgage.

Counteroffer: When the seller responds to the buyer's offer asking for changes in the offer such as price or contingencies. The buyer may then offer their counteroffer if they want to make changes to the seller's counteroffer.

County Recorder: Maintains and preserves county land records, deeds, mortgages, any type of information that is intended to be public record.

Credit Score: A FICO® score is the score given by the credit reporting agencies (TransUnion®, Equifax®, and Experian®) that is determined by a formula of open tradelines (credit cards, charge cards, auto loans, etc.), payment history, balances to credit limits, and bankruptcies, and charge-offs/collections.

Debt-to-income Ratio (DTI): This is the ratio between a person's gross pay per month versus the amount of their monthly payments. There are two types:

1) Front-end ratio indicates what portion of an individual's income is used to make mortgage payments. It is calculated as an individual's monthly housing expenses divided by his/her monthly gross income and is expressed as a percentage. Lenders use the front-end ratio in conjunction with the back-end ratio to determine how much a borrower can afford to borrow.

2) Back-end ratio indicates what portion of an individual's income is used to make mortgage and debt service payments (credit cards, auto, etc). It is calculated as an individual's monthly housing expenses plus his/her monthly debt service, divided by his/her monthly gross income and is expressed as a percentage. Monthly gross income is annual income before taxes, insurance, retirement, etc are deducted, divided by 12 (months). ("Adjusted gross income" on Federal Tax Returns and/or "wages, tips, other compensation" (box #1) on W2s are sometimes used for annual income)

Deed of Trust: A document that conveys title to a property which identifies three parties: The Trustor (the borrower); The Trustee (the party holding "bare or legal" title usually the title company); The Beneficiary (lender). It also identifies the loan amount, legal description of property securing the loan, the parties involved, the inception and maturity date, provisions of the mortgage and requirements, late fees, and legal procedures or remedies, acceleration and alienation clauses, riders identifying clauses such as prepayment penalties or terms of an adjustable mortgage. This document is recorded at the County Recorder's Office.

Default: The failure to fulfill the promise to repay the loan in a timely and agreed upon manner.

Disclosure: A written statement detailing for the buyer all information regarding the physical property involved in the transaction including any known defects, needed repairs, etc of the property.

Also, any document which details any fact that the parties to a transaction need to know in order to make an informed decision or may impact the transaction or their decision making.

Documentation Types for Loans:

1) Full is when all required documents are provided to substantiate income, assets, and employment.

2) Alternative is when the documents are used without confirmation from third parties such as VOE (verification of employment) or VOD (verification of deposits).

3) Stated Income/Stated Assets or No Doc is when the buyer states his/her income without any proof or documentation (these types of loans are no longer readily available and are rumored to be outlawed in the near future).

Down Payment: The amount invested by the borrower to lower the amount of the loan on the purchase of a home. This is required by most lenders to ensure that the borrower has at least some of his/her own money invested. The amount required by the lender is determined by factors such as FICO® score, assets, type of loan, type of property, and others.

Down Payment Assistance Programs (DAP)/First-time Home Buyer Programs: Programs offered, usually by a government entity, for down payment and closing cost assistance for low income borrowers.

Due Diligence: Where the buyer uses a specific period of time to inspect, appraise, and research factors influencing the livability of a property.

Dual Agency: When a real estate broker/agent represents both the buyer and the seller.

Easement: The right held by another property owner, business or government entity to use a portion of a person's property for a specific purpose.

Effective Interest Rate: The actual annual interest rate of the note after all discounting, fees, and points have been paid.

Eligibility: Citizenship/Immigration Status:
    a) U.S. Citizen
    b) Permanent Resident Alien (Green Card)
    c) Non-permanent Resident Alien
    d) Non-resident Alien

Encumbrance: This is a lien (claim) or burden on a property.

Equity: The difference between the value of a property

and the outstanding indebtedness secured by the property.

Fannie Mae (Federal National Mortgage Association): A private corporation licensed and regulated by the Federal Government which buys mortgage loans.

Fee Simple: The highest form of property ownership. It includes all property rights.

FHA Approved Condo Complex: A condo complex which has met FHA guidelines and is approved for an FHA loan.

FHA 203k Loan: Allows funds to rehabilitate a property.

FHA (Federal Housing Administration): The government agency that provides federal insurance for mortgage loans.

FHA Loan: A loan guaranteed by FHA only requiring (at the time of this publication) a down payment of 3.5%. There is an added fee (called pre-paid mortgage insurance) to help pay for the costs FHA incurs for administration. PMI (mortgage insurance) is required.

FICO® (Fair Isaac Corporation): (see "credit score")

Fiduciary: This is a standard of care that is held by someone who is acting on the behalf of another person. This includes acting in good faith, with loyalty and honesty, without seeking undue personal gain and without bias.

Foreclosure: The process where a lender will go through the legal process of repossessing a home due to a default of the loan payments. In the real estate/loan business these are often referred to as REOs (real estate owned).

Freddie Mac (Federal Home Loan Mortgage Corporation): A private corporation licensed and regulated by the Federal Government which buys mortgage loans.

Fully Amortized: When the payment includes the monthly interest charge and enough principal to ensure that the loan will be paid off during the term of the loan.

Ginnie Mae (GNMA-Government National Mortgage Association): This is a government agency supervised by HUD. It promotes investment by guaranteeing payment on FHA, FMHA, and VA Loans.

Grant: In reference to mortgages it usually refers to government programs which give first-time homebuyer assistance in the form of a loan which can be applied to down payment and/or closing costs and is forgiven after a specified time in which the homebuyer lives in the home.

Grant Deed: A document used to transfer ownership of a property. Mainly used in the western states.

Good Faith Deposit: An amount of money offered in conjunction with a purchase contract to be used as "security" to show that the offer is made in "good faith". This is usually held by the agent/broker or escrow until the buyer has done their "due diligence" such as inspections, appraisals, pest inspections, etc and makes a decision whether or not to continue the purchase process of the property. If the buyer decides not to buy the property within an agreed upon time period the good faith deposit is usually returned to the buyer.

Good Faith Estimate: This is a report with all of the financial details of a loan transaction such as the loan amount, interest rate, lender charges, lender/broker fees, closing costs, escrow fees, title fees, etc. This is a required disclosure.

Hazard Insurance: Insurance which covers the repair or replacement of property which has been destroyed by fire or natural occurrence. Often it will also cover other property related losses such as theft, vandalism, or some forms of litigation or property liability exposure.

Home Owner's Association (HOA): This is an association of home owners or condo owners when there is a common interest in either the property on which the buildings are built and/or common areas such as roads, club houses, swimming pools, etc. The condo owners usually vote on a board which determines how the HOA funds will be allocated and how the property is managed.

Home Owner's Association Dues (HOA fees): These are fees paid by the home/condo owners to help pay for the maintenance of the common areas and buildings in the association. Sometimes they cover things like trash removal, cable, and security. Often they cover replacement of roofs, pest control, and outside building maintenance.

Home Warranty Insurance: This is insurance which is paid at the end of escrow to insure the appliances, heating and cooling system, plumbing, electrical, and other designated physical items on the property after the buyer takes possession, usually for the first year but can be extended. Most often the premium is paid by the seller for the first year.

HUD 1 and Estimated HUD 1: These are statements that list the costs, finance amounts, and expenses in the purchase and loan transaction. These are prepared by escrow.

Impounds: Reserve accounts held in an escrow account and administered by the loan servicer to pay for recurring property taxes and hazard insurance premiums.

Index: This is the base by which ARM rates are determined. An index is used along with a margin established by the lender to determine what the ARM note rate will be. As the index changes, so does the interest rate. The indices change periodically. How often they change is dependent upon the index used and terms of the loan. The major forms are:

T-Bill-Treasury Bill
MTA or **MAT**-12 month Treasury Average
CODI-Certificate of Deposit Index
COFI-11th District Cost of Funds Index
COSI-Cost of Savings Index

LIBOR-London Inter Bank Offering Rates
CD-Certificates of Deposits Index
CMT or TCM-Constant Maturity Treasury
Prime Rate or Bank Prime Rate-Best rate offered by banks to their preferred corporate/business clients.

Insurance Binder: (See "Binder")

Insurance Certification: A document stating that the insurer is insuring a particular property.

Insurance Declaration: This is the first page of a policy which indicates the coverage of the policy. Every time a policy is renewed or updated a new "Dec page" is added.

Interest Only Loan: A loan which allows the payments to be made without paying down the principal and only paying the interest due.

Interest Rate Cap: The maximum rate of interest that can be charged on an ARM loan outlined in the note.

Lien: A recorded claim against a property to secure a loan, judgment, or other claim against the property. These claims must be satisfied in some form or fashion before the property can be transferred to another owner or the new owner must be willing to assume those claims.

Listing Agent/Seller's Agent: A real estate agent representing the seller of a property.

Loan Origination: The act of making a new loan.

Loan Servicer: An entity that performs administrative functions on a loan such as collecting the payments, etc. This may or may not be the original lender or investor for that loan.

LTV (Loan to Value): This is the amount that has or will be financed expressed as a percentage of the total value/purchase price of the property. (e.g.: Purchase price = $100,000; loan amount = $60,000; LTV = 60%.) **CLTV:** Means combined-loan-to-value. The total LTV when there are two or more loans on the property. (e.g.: 1st mortgage = $100,000 added to 2nd mortgage = $50,0000; total mtg: $150,000; purchase price/value = $200,000; CLTV = 75%.)

Margin: The number of points added to the index in order to determine the interest rate on an ARM (adjustable rate mortgage).

Maturity: The date that the contracted term of the loan has been/will be met.

Mechanic's Lien: A lien applied to personal property or real estate by a contractor or repair person who has performed work on that property and has not been paid.

Mello Roos: A tax on the property in addition to the normal property taxes in order to pay for the additional community services that are required by the building of new homes.

Mortgage: An instrument where the property is

pledged as security for a debt, creating a lien on the secured property and recorded with the county recorder's office.

Mortgage Insurance (MI) [Also called Private Mortgage Insurance (PMI)]**:** This is insurance on the mortgage in case of default by the borrower and is usually paid by the borrower in the form of monthly payments. This is for the benefit of the lender.

Multiple Listing Service (MLS): A listing service in which agents/Realtors® can view all of the listed properties available throughout a designated area (usually an entire county plus some adjacent counties or cities).

Neg-am (Negative Amortization): Negative amortization payments are when the minimum monthly payment is less than the amount of the interest charged each month. The remaining interest is accrued and added to the principal.

Nominal Interest Rate: This is the interest rate stated on the loan.

Occupancy Types: Owner-occupied, non-owner occupied/investment, 2nd home (vacation home).

Origination Fee: This is a fee charged by banks and brokers (not by all banks or other lenders) as a fee to cover costs for doing the loan. If an origination fee is not charged there are usually other ways the lender recovers costs from the borrower.

Pad: An amount of money added to the estimated HUD1 to ensure that there are enough funds from the buyer to cover unexpected costs at the close of escrow; usually around $350. If these funds are not used they are returned to the buyer after the close of escrow.

Parcel Number or Property Tax Map Code: Is a code used by the local governments to identify a specific property by using parcel numbers and plat map numbers.

Payment Cap: A limit on the increase in the monthly payment for each adjustment period on an ARM.

Permanent Financing: This term in real estate usually refers to a mortgage loan that is issued subsequent to a short term construction loan which is used just for the construction phase of a property.

PITI: This is an acronym for "principal, interest, taxes, and insurance". This is the sum of all items composing your monthly payment (excluding HOA fees).

Plat Map: A map of a subdivision outlining the individual parcels, size of the parcels, roads, and easements of that subdivision.

Pocket Listing: A property listing by an agent that is not advertised or placed on the MLS usually in order to save it for a special client or to allow the agent to obtain the buyer and make the commission for both sides of the transaction.

(Discount) Points: These are fees to buy down the

interest rate, either permanently or temporarily, to a lower rate.

Pre-paid Interest: This is the interest that is charged to the borrower to cover the time between the closing of escrow and the day the first full payment is due. It is charged per day. (e.g.: If the interest rate is 5% on a loan amount of $100,000 the daily interest would be $13.89/day. If escrow is closed on the 15th of the month and there are 15 days left in the month, the pre-paid interest charge would be $208.35.)

Pre-payment Penalty: A penalty applied when the loan is paid off early, usually within the first two to three years. These penalties can be substantial so it is wise to check the note before signing, selling, or refinancing. These are not normally applied to fixed loans but are usually included in ARM (adjustable rate) loans.

Pre-qualification and Pre-approval: A pre-qualification is a loan qualification which uses financial information about the borrower obtained verbally from the borrower and which has not been substantiated by documentation. This is usually used to preliminarily determine if the borrower should be taken to the next step of pre-approval and to approximate how much the borrower can afford to buy a house.

A pre-approval is when a credit report has been pulled and supporting documents have been used to qualify the borrower for a loan.

Qualifying is primarily based on, but not limited to:

31

- A ratio between your gross income per month and the amount of monthly debt service (DTI).
- Credit Score (FICO®)
- Loan to Value (LTV) (What portion of the value of the home is financed)

Principal: The amount borrowed on a loan.

Promissory Note: This is a document secured by the Deed of Trust and is the evidence of debt. This is signed by the borrower promising to repay the debt.

Property Management Company: A company that provides services to a homeowner's association such as maintenance, fee collection, bookkeeping, etc.

Property Tax: A tax based on an assessed value of the property by the tax assessor usually due in two installments over the year (depending on the municipality). These can (sometimes required) be paid monthly by paying into an escrow account managed by a loan servicing entity or lender.

Prorate: This term is used when a fee or tax is divided, distributed, or calculated to proportionately apply a division of those fees or taxes to a buyer and seller on an accrual basis.

Rate and Term Refinance: This is a refinance of a mortgage to change the interest rate and/or term of the loan with no additional cash added.

Rate Lock: This enables you to lock the interest rate for a specific period of time allowing you to be sure that you are getting the rate you are comfortable with. Rates can change several times a day so it is wise to ask the loan officer about trends and advice on when you should lock. No one can accurately predict what the lowest rate will be within a certain time period so don't expect it from your loan officer. It's always just an educated guess. Always ask the loan officer how long the rate is locked for. Extensions to the lock are usually possible for an additional fee.

Realtor®: Someone who belongs to the professional organization known as Realtors®. There are state, local, and national organizations of Realtors®. They regulate and provide services to member real estate agents to ensure the highest level of expertise and service in the real estate sales industry.

Right of Rescission: The right of a borrower to refuse the loan. For refinances there is a three day right of rescission. This allows the borrower(s) to change their mind up to three days after signing loan docs. This is a Federal law.

REO: See "Foreclosure".

Short Sale: This is the process of an owner selling a home which is, in most cases, in jeopardy of foreclosure and which has a market value less than the amount of the loan(s) on the property. The seller asks the lender to accept less than the amount owed on the mortgage(s). This can be a long process in that it often takes the approval and agreement of more than one lending or decision making entity.

Silent Seconds: Second mortgages, usually government offered down payment assistance programs, which do not require a monthly payment for the term of the loan. These are usually balloon loans (require full payment after a specified time period) that accrue simple interest over the life of the loan. Sometimes these loans are forgiven if the borrower lives on the property for a specified period of time.

Simple Interest: Interest calculated as a percentage of the principal only.

Subdivision: An area of land that has been divided into parcels usually for building homes or commercial property.

Subordinate Financing: A loan that takes second position behind another mortgage lien. (If there is a default on the loan the lender of the second is willing to try to recover their loan amount after the lender on the first mortgage recovers their loan amount)

Title Insurance: This insurance is a means of ensuring that the property is free and clear of encumbrances when the new owner takes possession.

Trust: Is a legal entity which can contain a person's or persons' assets which allows those assets to be controlled by a trustee after the death of the person or persons. This prevents the assets from having to go through probate and being controlled by a will or a judge. There are also tax benefits from having assets in a trust. Trusts are very complex and there are many types of trusts. They should be initiated only after consultation with a CPA or lawyer who specializes in trusts.

Trustee: A person or entity that holds property in trust for another. This is a fiduciary relationship.

Trustor: The person or entity that creates a trust.

Truth in Lending: The Truth in Lending Act of 1968 is a law intended to protect consumers by requiring the lender to disclose all costs and terms and conditions of the loan such as the APR, total amount paid if carried to the full term of the loan, loan amount, etc.

VA (Veteran Administration) Loan: This is a loan offered by the VA for Veterans and active duty military in order to make it easier for them to get a purchase loan and refinance their loans. This requires a zero down payment and no mortgage insurance is required. There are additional fees paid to the VA for their costs of doing the loan. The borrower must get a certificate of eligibility from the VA.

Vesting (types of ownership):

a) Sole Ownership: Usually single individual
b) Co-ownership (community property): Married persons and possibly civil unions.
c) Joint Tenancy: Married persons/partners
d) Tenants in Common: Married persons/partners
e) Revocable Trust: Kind of like a corporation. A legal separate entity to protect property from types of litigation and probate.
f) Corporation: Acts as a legal individual to protect property from types of litigation and taxes.
g) Partnership: Usually acts like an LLP (limited liability partnership).

35

h) Community Property with Right of Survivorship: Special tax rules for married persons to lessen the impact of inheritance taxation.

i) D.B.A.: Doing Business As...like owning a business for income properties.

j) Separate and Sole Ownership: Married people owning property as their sole and separate property.

Zoning: This is a governmental entity designating an area or areas for a specific use such as residential, business, agriculture, manufacturing, etc. These are often expressed with codes such as R1 for residential, 1 unit or "C" for commercial.

APPENDIX

Types of Loans:

Most popular loans:

a) Fixed Loan: A loan which has a fixed, or constant interest rate for a specified time period such as a 30 year   fixed, 40 year fixed, 20 year fixed, 15 year fixed.
b) Adjustable Rate Mortgage (ARM): This is a loan in which the interest rate adjusts at set time periods based on a mortgage index plus a margin.

Other loans, sub-loan categories, and loans which are no longer available or not widely used:

a) Interest Only: a period where a monthly payment of the interest only is allowed.
b) 3/1, 5/1, 7/1, 10/1 ARM (Hybrid loans): Loans that have an initial fixed term followed by a remaining period of adjustable rates.
c) Option ARM: Loans with payment options allowed. (e.g.: negative amortization, interest only, fully amortized, accelerated payment) (see glossary)
d) Combo Loan (piggyback loan): A loan that is originated by a single lender done in two loans, a

I

first and second mortgage, to avoid the necessity of mortgage insurance. First loans in excess of 80% LTV must have mortgage insurance.

e) HELOC (Equity line of credit): This is a line of credit secured by property and is used similarly to a credit card (revolving line of credit) usually at lower interest rates than a credit card.

f) HELOAN (Home equity loan): Similar to a second mortgage.

g) 1st Mortgage: A lien placed against a property that has the legal right to be paid before any other liens.

h) 2nd Mortgage: A lien placed against a property that is paid (upon foreclosure) after the 1st lien holder.

i) Conforming Loan: A loan of $417,000 or under which conforms to Fannie Mae and Freddie Mac guidelines.

j) Non Conforming (Jumbo): At the time of this publication there are two types of loans above $417,000. They are Conforming Jumbo loans which are loan amounts between $417,000 and an amount that is determined by area, but with the maximum allowed for Conforming Jumbo at $625,500. Jumbo are loans above the $625,500. At each level there are different interest rates charged with the lowest rate being for the conforming loan.

k) Commercial Loans: These are loans that are used for investment/commercial properties and for residential properties that consist of more than 4 units.

l) Conventional Loans: These are loans that are not backed by FHA (Federal Housing Administration) or VA (Veteran's Administration). These can however, be guided by rules of Fannie Mae or Freddie Mac.

m) LMI: This is in reference to loans that require the

borrower to be qualified under standards that designate them as low to middle income borrowers.

n) Stated Income Loan (SISA, NINA): These are loans that require no verification of income. SISA is a stated income loan that does not require proof of assets. NINA is a loan that does not require information on income or assets.

o) Lot Loan: There are two basic types of these loans. One is where the lot is part of a subdivision and can have roads and utilities available. The other is a lot which is raw land and may or may not have some utilities available.

p) Construction Loan: A loan to supply the money for constructing the building(s) and sometimes to buy the lot. These loans usually require conversion to a permanent mortgage loan after completion of the building.

q) First Time Homebuyer Loans: Loans with special guidelines to make it easier for first-time homebuyers to qualify for a home (usually defined as someone who has not owned a home for 3 years).

r) Silent Seconds: This is when monthly payments are deferred or not required for a specified amount of time.

s) Wrap Around Loan (All inclusive deed of trust): When a prior loan on the property is assumed along with obtaining another loan for the balance of the purchase price.

Types of Homes:

a) Single Family Residence (SFR): One detached unit intended to house one family usually on separately owned property.

b) Townhouse/Row House: An attached residence that is usually two or more levels which is on property that can either be owned by the resident or part of a community owned lot.

c) Condominium: Single level residence attached to other units with a shared interest in the land the building sits on generally managed by a homeowner's association. These can be either low-rise or high-rise buildings.

d) 2 to 4 units: These units can either be attached or separate buildings built on one lot and sold as a whole. Over 4 units are considered as commercial property and must be financed as such.

e) Apartments over 4 units: These are condo-like units that are generally rented out by a single owner of all the units. However, there are some areas that do have apartments that are owned by individuals.

f) Mobile Home: Pre-built units built on axles transported on wheels to the location and then put on a raised foundation. Usually classified as a vehicle licensed by the DMV.

g) Manufactured Home: Pre-built and then transported to location placed on a permanent foundation and classified as property.

h) Pre-fabricated Home or Modular Home: Built in sections at a manufacturing site then transported to the property and assembled.

i) Condominium Hotel or Condotel: These are condos with amenities like a hotel such as room service, concierge, etc.

j) Loft: Usually one large room that is sectioned off for different living areas. Usually on a level above the first floor.

k) PUD (planned unit development): These can be

condos, townhomes, or SFRs. They are in a single community (subdivision) with the land being owned by the owner of the unit but usually pays a fee to help maintain the common areas and are part of a home owner's association (HOA).
l) Co-operative: Like apartments but are individually owned.
m) Log Homes: Homes built out of whole logs.
n) Dome or Geodesic Dome Homes: Built in the form of a dome or several domes that are attached by breezeways or rooms. These are often pre-fabricated or are in the form of kits.

A typical document and information list for completing a loan.

Not all items will be applicable for all borrowers. Additional documentation may be required depending on the type of loan and each individual's special circumstances.

The following is an application checklist. Use this checklist to make sure you have compiled all required information. The more information you provide the easier the loan transaction.

___Last two years of tax returns with all schedules **signed**). (State return not needed)

___ Payroll check stubs covering the last 30 days/1 month.

___ W-2 from all current and past employers for last 2 years.

____ Last 2 months of bank statements, all pages, (checking and savings) and investment accounts. They must have your name and account number on them.

___Copy of bankruptcy discharge (if applicable).

___ Information on all Real Estate owned. Copy of last mortgage statement (Value, loan balance, loan payment, rent $)

____If you are a landlord have a copy of your leases or at least the amounts of your rental income.

____Landlord's name, address and <u>telephone #</u>.

____Copy of Driver's License and Social Security Card (Green card if you have one).

____Statement with:
- □ Employer's name, address, **phone number**
- □ How many years on job (if less than 2yrs; need <u>complete</u> info on previous employer)
- □ How many years in occupation (dates beginning and end)
- □ Year and Make of Automobiles and approximate value
- □ Any spousal or child support—received or paid
- □ Years of schooling
- □ Number of Dependents and their ages
- □ Current Rent/Payments, property taxes, insurance, HOA fees, MELLO ROOS
- □ Previous address(es) and landlord info if not at current address for more than 2 yrs
- □ Real Estate taxes (if applicable)

- ☐ HOA fees (if applicable)
- ☐ Homeowner's Insurance Premium (if applicable)
- ☐ Bank accounts: Account numbers, bank name, and address
- ☐ Asset list and account numbers and documentation) (CD's, stocks, bonds, life insurance, 401K, etc)

For more information or clarification on subjects covered in this book go to www.thenutshellbook.com.

www.ingramcontent.com/pod-product-compliance
Lightning Source LLC
Chambersburg PA
CBHW051251170526
45165CB00004B/1673